THE ABDUCTION PREVENTION LIBRARY™

# STAYING SAFE BY SAYING NO

Cynthia MacGregor

The Rosen Publishing Group's
PowerKids Press™
New York

Published in 1999 by The Rosen Publishing Group, Inc.
29 East 21st Street, New York, NY 10010

First Edition

Book Design: Danielle Primiceri

Photo Illustrations: Cover by Carrie Anne Grippo ; pp. 4, 7, 8, 11, 12, 15, 16, 19, 20 © Donna M. Scholl.

MacGregor, Cynthia.
    Staying safe by saying no/ by Cynthia MacGregor.
        p.    cm. — (The abduction prevention library)
    Includes index.
    Summary: Explains the significance of saying "no" in potentially dangerous situations, particularly with strangers.
    ISBN 0-8239-5252-5
    1. Children and strangers—Juvenile literature. 2. Abduction—Prevention—Juvenile literature.
    3. Child sexual abuse—Prevention—Juvenile literature. [1. Strangers. 2. Safety.
    3. Child sexual abuse.] I. Title. II. Series.
HQ784.S8M368 1998
613.6'083—DC21                                                            97-53216
                                                                              CIP
                                                                               AC

Manufactured in the United States of America

# Contents

# Is Yes Always the Right Word?

We all want to be **cooperative** (koh-AH-prah-tiv) and helpful. Most of us want to be polite too. When someone asks for help, we want to help that person. If someone **offers** (OFF-erz) us something, we want to be able to **accept** (ak-SEPT) it. That's true whether we're offered a cookie, a ride home, or a chance to visit our friends. We want to say yes to all these things. But sometimes it's safer to say no.

*It can be hard to know what to do if something is offered to you, especially by a stranger.*

# Sometimes No Is a Safer Word

If someone asks you for **directions** (dih-REK-shunz) to Elm Street, he probably does want to know where the street is. But you never know for sure. That person might actually be up to no good. He or she may want to harm you. What's the safest thing to do? Say no. The person can always find a police officer or another adult to ask for directions.

*Run away if you say no to someone asking for directions and the person keeps trying to talk to you.* ▶

# A Long Walk

Jeremy was walking home. A car pulled up beside him. The driver was someone Jeremy had seen a few times before. He worked with Jeremy's dad. "I'm going toward your house. Do you want a ride?" the man asked.

Jeremy was tired. He didn't really want to walk. But he remembered what his parents had taught him. He knew he was only supposed to accept rides with certain people. This man wasn't one of these people. "No thanks," Jeremy said. "I don't mind walking."

◀ *Don't stick around to talk to a person who offers you a ride. Instead, leave quickly.*

# Sneaky Tricks

Brian and Shawna were playing outside after school. A woman walked up to them.

"Have you kids ever done any modeling?" she asked. The kids said no. "Would you like to be in my magazine? I'm taking pictures a few blocks from here," the woman said.

"Yes!" Brian said. "What do you think, Shawna?"

Shawna didn't know this woman. "No thanks," Shawna said. "Let's go, Brian."

Shawna and Brian left quickly. Shawna made the right **decision** (dih-SIH-zhun).

*No matter how cool or interesting an offer might sound, say no if you don't know that person.* ▶

# Strange Questions

Adam was playing a computer game on-line. He went into a **chat room** (CHAT ROOM) by mistake. Someone started typing messages to Adam. He said his name was Rick and that he was fourteen. Adam thought it was neat that an older boy wanted to talk to him. Rick started asking Adam questions. Rick wanted to know what Adam looked like and where he lived. This made Adam **uncomfortable** (un-KUMF-ter-buhl). Rick kept asking. But Adam typed "no" and left the chat room right away. Adam did the right thing.

◀ *Using a computer can be a fun way to learn. But your safety comes first.*

# A Package

Erin got home from school right before her mom got home from work. The doorbell rang just after Erin got there. Erin saw a deliveryman through the window. And he saw Erin.

"I have a package for your mom," he said.

"Please leave it at the door," Erin said.

"You have to sign for it," the man said. "Open the door."

"No," Erin said loudly. "Come back later."

The man left.

Later, Erin's mom told her that she did the right thing.

*No matter how important a package or message may be, the person delivering it can always come back or call later.* ▶

# A Friend of Mom's ?

Jimmy was playing ball in the yard. A man drove up in a van. "Hi, Jimmy," the man said. Jimmy didn't **recognize** (REH-kig-nyz) him.

"Don't you remember me?" the man asked. "I'm Bill, a friend of your mom's. My dog Scooter just had puppies. They're at my house. Do you want to see them?"

Jimmy wanted to see the puppies. But he didn't know this man.

"No thanks," Jimmy said. Even if Bill was one of his mom's friends, Jimmy knew he was doing the right thing.

◀ *Someone who says he's a friend of your mom's might be telling the truth, but how well do **you** know him?*

# Cookies

Mr. Mason, the new neighbor, was in his yard when Sam walked by.

"Hi, Sam," Mr. Mason said. "Come in and have some cookies. I just baked them."

Sam's mom had taught him about strangers and being safe. Sam knew he shouldn't go into a stranger's house, even if it was a neighbor. Mr. Mason seemed like a nice man. But Sam didn't know him very well. Sam said, "No, thanks," and kept walking toward his house.

*Your new neighbor is probably a very nice person. But until you know him better, think about safety first.* ▶

# "Our Little Secret"

Mr. Stone owned a store near Lisa's house. One day Lisa was in the store. Mr. Stone said, "I have a turtle behind the counter. Would you like to see it?"

Lisa said yes. Mr. Stone let Lisa peek at the turtle behind the counter.

"Come back on Saturday, and I'll let you hold the turtle," Mr. Stone said. "But don't tell anyone. This will be our secret."

Lisa didn't like the sound of that at all. "No," Lisa said. She went right home and told her parents. And she didn't go back to the store.

◀ *Grown-ups like Mr. Stone can usually be trusted. But isn't it better to be safe than to put yourself in danger?*

# A Survey

Danny was home alone when a man called on the phone. "I'm taking a survey," he said. Being asked for help made Danny feel important. One of the questions was, "Do both of your parents work?"

Danny almost said yes. Then he realized that saying yes would tell this stranger that he was home alone. Danny wanted to be safe. So he said, "No. Good-bye," and hung up.

Sometimes you have to say no in **situations** (SIT-choo-AY-shunz) that make you uncomfortable. Be smart: Think first and say no if you think it will keep you safe.

# Glossary

**accept** (ak-SEPT)  To take.

**chat room** (CHAT ROOM)  An on-line site, or program, where people can type messages to each other.

**cooperative** (koh-AH-prah-tiv)  Helpful and easy to get along with.

**decision** (dih-SIH-zhun)  To make up your mind about something.

**direction** (dih-REK-shun)  Help given to someone on how to get to a certain place.

**offer** (OFF-er)  To want to give something to someone.

**recognize** (REH-kig-nyz)  To know someone or something.

**situation** (SIT-choo-AY-shun)  A problem; an event that happens.

**uncomfortable** (un-KUMF-ter-buhl)  Feeling scared and unsure of yourself.

# Index